HOW THEY LIVE

WHALES

RAY GAMBELL

MALLARD PRESS

A Southern Right
Whale with its
characteristic
V-shaped blow.

Contents

Introduction

Advances in modern technology and equipment have meant that we have learned a great deal more about whales in recent years, and yet much is still mysterious about these magnificent creatures. At first, they seem to have little in common with us, but there are in fact close similarities. For instance, they too are mammals with large brains who live in complex social groupings. Many species of whales were once in danger of being hunted to extinction by Man, but that danger has largely passed and some at least are increasing again. It will be a test of humanity's intelligence and ability to co-operate internationally to ensure that whales continue to thrive in the oceans of the world.

Whales are mammals – they are warm-blooded, breathe air, and the females give birth to live young which feed on their mother's milk for the first months of their lives. These are rather surprising features to find in animals which spend their whole lives in the sea, but whales have become very much modified from their early land-living ancestors.

Whales and their close relatives, the dolphins and porpoises, are known as *cetaceans*. The very earliest cetaceans appeared some 50 million years ago, having evolved from small amphibious mammals. They were quite small and still had four short legs, but gradually they evolved into streamlined creatures looking somewhat like a modern dolphin. These earliest whales died out about 25 million years ago, leaving the two groups of modern whales, the baleen whales and the toothed whales.

The great whales, such as the Blue, Humpback and Right Whales, are all baleen whales. They have no teeth in their great bowed jaws, but a row of horny fibrous plates – the *baleen* or whalebone – hanging from the upper jaws at each side of the mouth. This is used to filter from the water

small shrimp-like crustaceans known as krill and other plankton.

The toothed whales, which also include the dolphins and porpoises, are generally smaller, the Sperm Whale being the largest representative of this group.

Amongst the toothed whales, the Killer Whale, the Bottlenose Whale and the beaked whales are all of medium size, whereas the various dolphin species are smaller. The dolphins include a small group of very specialized freshwater species known as river dolphins. Other members of the toothed whales are the extraordinary Narwhal – the unicorn of the seas – with a long tusk projecting from the front of the upper jaw in males, and the White Whale or Beluga, which are found only in the Arctic. All toothed whales have a greater or lesser

The broad flukes of the tail show above the surface just before the Gray Whale dives.

number of teeth in their jaws for seizing their prey, usually fish or squid.

The great whales are all highly streamlined. The head merges into the body with no obvious neck but, in spite of their size, whales are surprisingly flexible in the water. The body is supported by a skeleton which is made up of all the usual mammalian bones, although these bones are lightweight and spongy compared to those of land mammals, containing a lot of fatty tissue which aids buoyancy.

The rear third of the body is flattened from side to side, with strong muscles that drive the up-and-down swimming movements of the tail. The flattened shape reduces drag against the water as the tail moves, and probably also helps stabilize the body. All species except the Right Whales have a fin or hump on the midline of the back, which may act as a keel to steady the

body and prevent it rolling too much.

The forelimbs have become modified into paddle-like flippers, with bones equivalent to those of a human hand and arm. The flippers help the whale to control the angle of its body, acting as stabilizers, and can also be used for steering, as the flipper can rotate at the shoulder. No hindlimbs are visible outside the body, as they have become much reduced in size and are usually represented only by a small bone buried deep in the muscles below the back.

The backbone extends right to the end of the body, but there are no bones in the flattened flukes of the tail, which is made up chiefly of hard fibrous tissue. The movements of the tail drive the animal through the water. The tail flukes of a whale are flattened horizontally and move up and down, in contrast to the vertical tail fins of a fish, which move from side to side.

The size and form of the great whales shows a range across the various species.

Sperm Whale
(*Physeter catodon*)

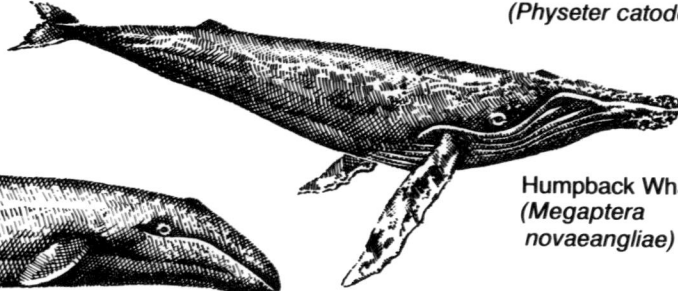

Humpback Whale
(*Megaptera novaeangliae*)

Gray Whale
(*Eschrichtius robustus*)

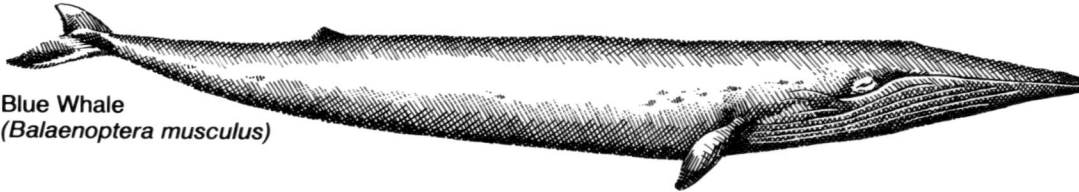

Blue Whale
(*Balaenoptera musculus*)

Fin Whale
(*Balaenoptera physalus*)

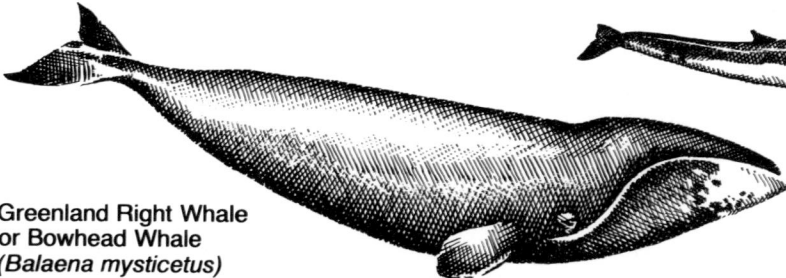

Minke Whale
(*Balaenoptera acutorostrata*)

Greenland Right Whale or Bowhead Whale
(*Balaena mysticetus*)

Only small numbers of the Northern Right Whale remain after excessive hunting in earlier centuries.

Baleen Whales

The Right Whales are so called because at one time they were the "right" ones to hunt. They were easy to chase and catch because they swim slowly, and also float at the surface when they are dead. Their long baleen plates and oil-rich blubber made them especially valuable and so the "right" prize for the whalers.

The Greenland Right Whale, or Bowhead (*Balaena mysticetus*), has a very large triangular head with an enormous mouth containing over 300 baleen plates each side, the longest over 4m (13ft) in length. The blubber is the thickest of all the whales. A full grown Bowhead can measure up to 20m (66ft) and weight 100 tons. The body is barrel-shaped, black nearly all over, except for some patches of white under the chin and grey on the flippers and near the tail. There is no fin on the back.

The Northern and Southern Right Whales (*Eubalaena glacialis* and *E. australis*) are very similar in appearance. They can grow to a size of 18m (59ft) and a weight of 90 tons. The skin is brown-black with irregular white patches on throat and belly. The most striking feature of these whales is the series of growths (callosities) on the top and sides of the head in front of the blowholes and around the mouth. The one on the front of the upper jaw is known as the bonnet. The arrangement of these areas of rough skin seems to vary in each whale, so that they can be individually recognized. As they swim slowly, the callosities provide a home for many worms and whale lice.

The Gray Whale (*Eschrichtius robustus*) is one of the most easily seen of the large whales, since it spends nearly all its time in shallow coastal waters along the Pacific coast of North America. Because it swims relatively slowly, barnacles are able to settle and grow on its skin, giving it a rather mottled appearance. There is a small fin set well back along the back, and a number of knobs and ridges further towards the tail. The males grow up to 13m (43ft) long and the females 14m (46ft), and weigh up to 39 tons. The newborn calf is a little less than 5m (16ft) long.

All the remaining baleen whales are rather similar in form, with a torpedo-like body and triangular fin placed far back towards the tail. They have a series of parallel grooves or pleats in the skin of the throat and chest. These grooves are normally held tightly into the throat so that the head appears sleek and narrowing towards the tip when viewed from the side. They are fast swimming, and tend to sink when dead, so that they only became prey to whalers in the last 100 years when modern catching methods allowed them to be successfully chased and secured. A general term for these whales is rorquals. Many of them have a worldwide distribution, with two separate populations, one in the Northern and one in the Southern Hemisphere. In all species, members of populations inhabiting the Southern Hemisphere grow a little larger than those in the North. Females also grow slightly bigger than the males.

Left: Patches of barnacles frequently attach themselves to the skin of the Gray Whale.

Below: The skeleton of a massive Blue Whale laid out on King George Island in the Antarctic.

Blue Whales (*Balaenoptera musculus*) are the largest animals in the world. They can grow up to 30m (nearly 100ft) long and attain a weight of over 150 tons. The Blue Whale is a distinctive mottled blue-grey, with some white spots on the belly. A sub-species was discovered in the 1960s which is paler and has a relatively shorter tail region with a longer trunk. This was called the Pygmy Blue Whale (*Balaenoptera musculus brevicauda*), although it still grows up to $24\frac{1}{2}$m (80ft) long, and seems to live parti-cularly in the southern Indian Ocean.

The Fin Whale (*Balaenoptera physalus*) is slightly smaller than the Blue Whale, reaching 25m (82ft) in length and a weight of 90 tons. It is grey above, grading to white below, and the undersides of the flippers and tail flukes are also white. The dark colour of the head is strikingly asymmetrical. The front of the lower jaw on the right is white

11

but on the left it is the usual grey. The baleen plates in the mouth have a similar colour pattern. The head is quite triangular in shape when seen from above, and there is a distinct ridge along the back behind the fin.

Sei Whales (*Balaenoptera borealis*) reach a maximum size of about 18m (60ft). They are dark grey with a bluish tinge, but white over the grooved throat area. There are often oval scar-like marks on the back and flanks, giving a somewhat marbled appearance. The back fin is relatively large and curved backwards.

Bryde's Whale (*Balaenoptera edeni*) is very similar to the Sei Whale, although slightly smaller, reaching 16m (52ft) in length and 27 tons in weight. These two species were often confused in earlier years. The most obvious way to distinguish them is

by the two prominent ridges running down the top of the head of the Bryde's Whale, on either side of the central ridge which occurs on both species.

The Minke Whale (*Balaenoptera acutorostrata*) is the smallest of the rorquals, reaching 11m (36ft) and 19 tons. The colour is black to dark grey on the back and white below. Minke Whales in the Northern Hemisphere have a diagonal band of white on the upper surface of each flipper. In the Southern Hemisphere this band is absent or appears only as a slight grey marking. In all forms the flipper is white underneath.

The Humpback Whale (*Megaptera novaeangliae*) is easily recognized by its very long flippers, which may reach almost a third of the body length of 16m (52ft). It is more rounded and bulky than the other rorquals, and can weigh up to 60 tons. In addition to irregular lumps on the flippers there are also protuberances on the head, particularly around the jaws. The colour is dark above and with a very variable amount of white below extending up the sides. The colour pattern on the underside of the tail also differs between individuals. The throat region has fewer pleats and folds than in the other rorquals. Barnacles attach to the skin, especially under the chin and on the flippers and tail flukes.

Toothed Whales

Unlike baleen whales, toothed whales are not filter feeders, but instead hunt their prey – mainly fish and squid – which they seize with their teeth. The Sperm Whale (*Physeter catodon*) is the largest of all in this class. It has a huge head which takes up one third of the 18m (nearly 60ft) total length of an adult male. The females are much smaller, seldom exceeding 11.5m (38ft) and with a relatively smaller head. The front of the head is made up of an oil reservoir, the *spermaceti organ*. This gives the whale a blunted square-headed look, although it is in fact still quite streamlined. The lower jaw is narrow and overhung by the head, with up to two dozen thick conical teeth on each side. These fit into sockets in the roof of the mouth, where a few small vestigial teeth may be exposed. There is a distinct hump on the back, rather than a fin, with a series of smaller humps on the midline further towards the tail. There is also a keel along the underside of the tail stock region. The body colour is dark grey brown, with occasional patches or flecks of white, particularly under the belly. The body has a corrugated or ridged appearance,

Minke Whales approach close to shore, and can breach clear of the water.

The narrow jaw under the blunt head is visible in this leaping Sperm Whale.

Opposite: A group of Gray Whales migrating along the Pacific coast of North America.

and there are often circular scars or scratches. These are though to be made by the hooks and suckers on the arms of the squid which is its main food.

The spermaceti organ is a large reservoir of spermaceti oil lying on the top of the skull of the sperm whale. There are two main sections, an upper "sac" containing oil in an extremely tough "case", and a lower "junk" divided into a series of block-like compartments. The function of this organ is not entirely clear, but there are three main possibilities. It may act as a reverberation chamber and acoustic lens to magnify and focus the clicks that are used for echolocation and possibly also to stun the Sperm Whale's prey.

It may also be concerned with the deep-diving capacity of the Sperm Whale, by absorbing nitrogen in the air from the lungs before it goes into the bloodstream.

The spermaceti organ may also act as a buoyancy regulator for deep diving. If the spermaceti oil is cooled it forms a clear wax whose density helps the whale to descend to the depths. After the whale has finished feeding on the bottom, the spermaceti can be warmed by blood flowing through blood vessels running in it. The spermaceti lightens as it turns to oil and so helps the whale to rise to the surface.

This one organ may indeed serve all three functions, and have several uses in the life of the whale. The commercial significance of spermaceti is that it solidifies on exposure to air and cold into a very fine wax which was used in earlier times for making the best quality candles.

Distribution and Migration

Whales can be found in all the world's oceans, from the edge of the polar ice to the Equator. The rorquals in particular show marked seasonal changes in distribution, occupying waters closer to the poles during the summer months in both Northern and Southern Hemispheres. During the winter they shift towards the tropics. This movement pattern is linked to the abundance of food in the polar seas in the summer, and the relative warmth and calm of the more equatorial waters in the winter when the whales are breeding and giving birth to their young. As the seasons are opposite in the Northern and Southern Hemispheres, the populations of whales do not move towards the Equator at the same time.

In all these species at least three geographically isolated populations are recognized – one in the North Atlantic, another in the North Pacific, and a third in the Southern Hemisphere. Each population is probably made up of several more or less separate sub-groups, although animals may move between these smaller units at different times in their lives. It is this rather slow mixing process which keeps all whales of a species looking more or less similar no matter where they are found in the world.

Blue and Minke Whales migrate right up to the ice-edge in the polar waters, although the Blue Whales do not go quite so far north in the North Pacific. It is generally the bigger and older animals which go to the highest latitudes. The older Blue Whales and the pregnant females tend to migrate to the feeding grounds in advance of the other groups of whales.

In the Southern Hemisphere the Fin Whales tend to enter and leave the Antarctic after the Blue Whales but before the Sei Whales. The bigger and older animals generally penetrate further south than the younger whales. Males tend to precede the females, with pregnant females

in front of the other females and immature whales at the rear of the stream.

Sei Whales do not go so far towards the polar waters as do the other rorquals, and their movements are somewhat more irregular than those of Blue and Fin Whales. The appearance of large numbers of Sei Whales on a particular whaling ground in the past, such as South Georgia or Iceland, was described as a "Sei Whale year".

Humpback Whales are also found in all the world's oceans, but unlike the other rorquals they come in close to the coast and breed in shallow waters. They spend about $5\frac{1}{2}$ months during the winter on the feeding grounds, and then take 4 months swimming to and from the breeding areas, with $1\frac{1}{2}$ months for breeding in the warmer waters.

The migrating stream of Humpback Whales in the Southern Hemisphere leaves the breeding grounds with the newly pregnant females in the lead. This is so that they can spend the maximum time on the feeding grounds, building up stored food reserves to help their young ones grow. They are then the last to leave the Antarctic at the end of the summer. Mothers with newborn calves are the last to leave the breeding grounds, but the first to set off northwards in the autumn.

Sperm Whales are widely distributed in all oceans, although they avoid the polar pack ice in both hemispheres. Sperm Whales tend to remain in deep water, but they are often found around submarine ridges or steeply shelving areas closer to land. Here the upwelling ocean currents provide a good food supply.

A distinctive feature of Sperm Whale distribution is that although the males can be found throughout the tropical and polar seas, the females are confined to the warmer waters and do not go into the cold waters of the higher latitudes.

Blue and Humpback Whales migrate regularly between their winter breeding areas and the summer feeding grounds in each hemisphere.

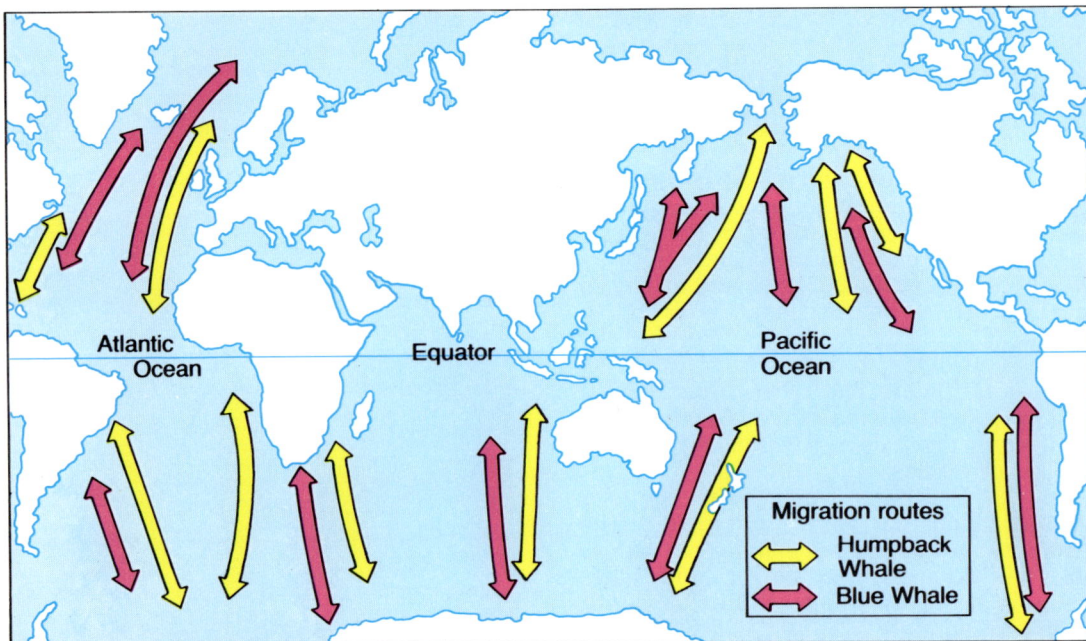

Atlantic Ocean

Equator

Pacific Ocean

Migration routes
Humpback Whale
Blue Whale

Nevertheless, groups of female Sperm Whales with their offspring, and the younger males in their separate groups, do move around with the seasons. Within tropical and warm temperate waters there is a general shift northwards during the northern summer and southern winter, and a southward return movement during the northern winter and southern summer. Because there does not seem to be any distinct separation between the Northern and Southern Hemisphere populations of Sperm Whales it seems possible that there is some exchange across the Equator. The large males spend the summer in the rich polar waters and then move towards the lower latitudes. There they compete among themselves to gain control over a harem of females and mate in the winter months.

The Gray Whale is found only in the Northern Hemisphere. There used to be Gray Whales in the North Atlantic until the 15th or 16th centuries, but they have died out, possibly through over-hunting in earlier centuries.

In the North Pacific there are two geographically distinct populations, one on the Asian and the other on the North American side. The Asian population is very small, and may be on the point of extinction. These whales migrate from their warm water breeding grounds around Korea to the Okhotsk Sea where they feed in the summer. Their continuing existence must be in doubt, because they have been seriously reduced in numbers by hunting in the past. In addition, their coastal breeding grounds and migration routes have been greatly affected by industrial development along the coasts and by shipping, which have very largely destroyed the conditions they require for breeding.

The situation of the Gray Whales on the North American coast is much more secure. They spend the winter in shallow lagoons along the coast of Baja California in

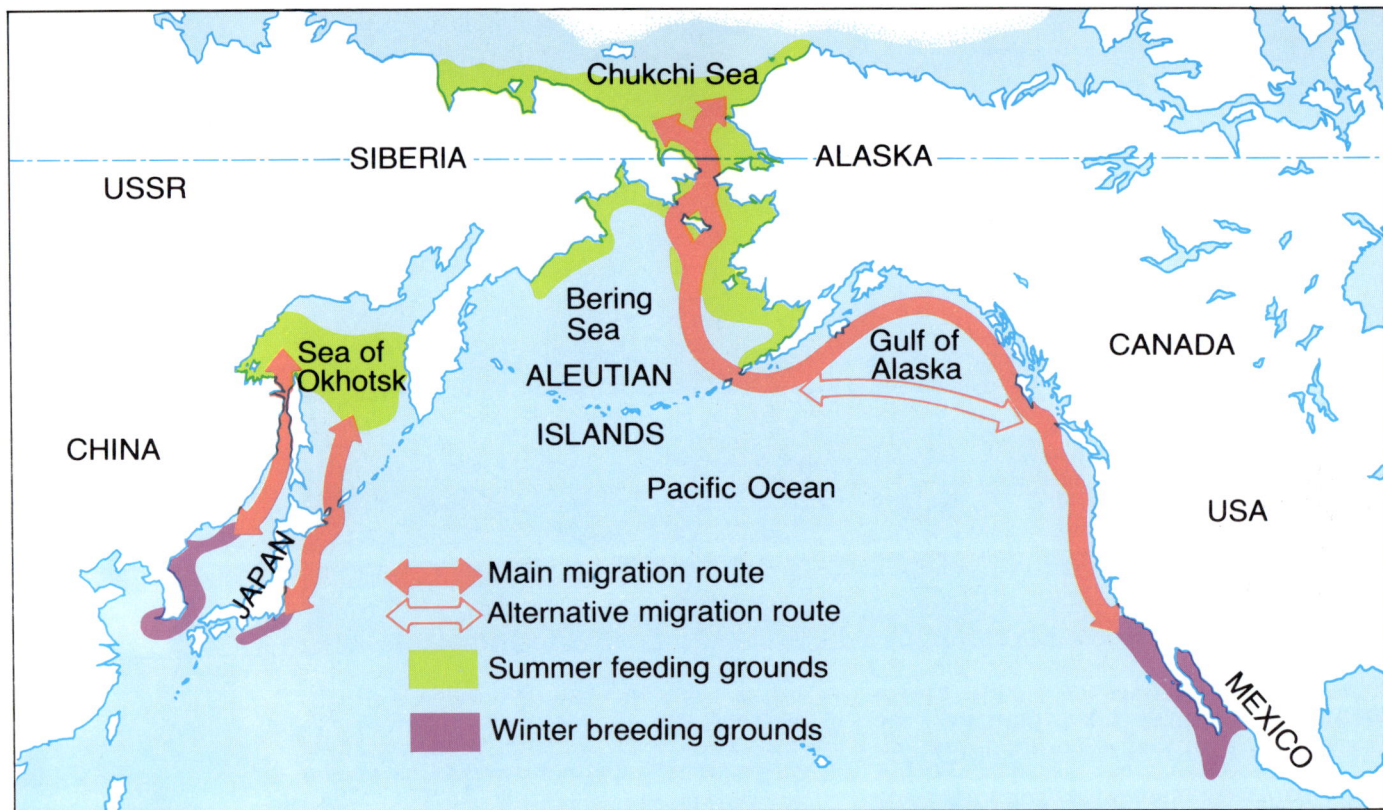

The migration routes of the Gray Whale are close to the coast in the North Pacific.

Mexico. There the adults mate and the females give birth to their calves before starting the longest annual migration of any mammal.

During the spring the Gray Whales swim northwards, generally within a few miles of the coast. They travel at a speed of about 5 mph (8km/h), and by summer have reached the polar feeding grounds. After passing through the narrow Bering Straits between Siberia and Alaska, they fan out into the Chukchi and Bering Seas where they feed during the long daylight hours of the northern summer. As the ice begins to freeze over the Arctic Ocean in autumn the whales start on their return journey to the warmer waters in the south. Travelling close to the

coast once more, they return to the breeding lagoons to complete the round trip of some 10,000 miles (16,000km) in a year.

While they are on migration Gray Whales have a very predictable pattern of breathing. They make three to five blows at intervals of 15 to 30 seconds before raising the tail flukes and submerging for 3 to 5 minutes. This very regular cycle is repeated again and again on both the southbound and northbound migrations.

The Bowhead (or Greenland Right Whale) is confined to the Arctic waters of the Northern Hemisphere. Sadly, these whales were nearly wiped out in the last century by over-catching. The only major population remaining is around the coast of

Alaska in the Bering Sea, with a few others in the Hudson Bay area of Canada.

In the spring as the ice starts to melt in the Bering Sea the Bowheads move northwards. They wait until the water is clear of solid ice between Alaska and Siberia and then pass through the Bering Strait and along the north coast of Alaska. The ice normally starts to crack open close to the coast, forming "leads" along which the Bowheads swim towards their feeding grounds in the Beaufort Sea.

Here the Bowheads will feed during the long Arctic summer days before the ice starts to thicken and press towards the shore once more in autumn. The Bowheads then migrate westwards and retrace their path back to the open waters of the Bering Sea for the winter.

Northern and Southern Right Whales occur worldwide except in tropical and Arctic waters. The populations in the Northern and Southern Hemispheres are separated from each other by the belt of tropical waters which they do not enter. These Right Whales too were much reduced in numbers by the catches a century or more ago, although some populations off Argentina and South Africa do seem to be increasing at last. In these two locations the Right Whales can be seen rather easily as they come close inshore to calve during winter and spring. Off Argentina at least, there seem to be three different populations which arrive in successive years to breed. Where the animals go in the intervening years is not known, but one whale has been recognized again around South Georgia.

19

Food and Feeding

The baleen whales are filter feeders. They
have developed very large mouths which
can take in great quantities of food. The
lower jaw is made up of two great bowed jaw
bones, and the skin of the throat region is
pleated in all except the Right Whales to
allow an even greater capacity when the
throat is distended. From the upper jaws
project a row of several hundred long
triangular plates. These are made of baleen,
a horny substance rather like stiff hair.
Indeed, the inner edges of the long plates are
fringed with hair-like fibres which act as the
filter through which the whale strains its
food.

Baleen is a living tissue rather like our
fingernails or hair, and continues to grow
throughout the lifetime of the whale. The tip
and outer edges are continously worn away
by the action of closing the mouth and
feeding, and the baleen plates are renewed
from the new growth at the gum.

The most abundant food in the oceans is
the plankton. This consists of vast quantities of drifting microscopic plants, and the
small animals which feed on them. These
animals are the main food of the whales.

The animal plankton occurs in enormous
quantities especially in the polar waters
where conditions are ideal for its production
and growth. During the long daylight hours
of summer the energy of the sun and the rich
nutrients in the polar waters combine to
create a seasonal bloom of plant plankton.
This in turn supports the animal plankton
which feeds on it. In the Antarctic Ocean
the predominant animal in the plankton is
the shrimp-like *krill*, which grows to a
length of about 5cm (2in). Krill form swarms
of many millions of individuals, which may
reach many hundreds of metres across in the
upper layers of the water where their plant
food is also most abundant.

The Blue, Fin, Minke and Humpback
Whales generally gulp their food. As these
whales swim through waters which are rich

A diagram of the
mouth of a baleen
whale. This functions
as a large filter for
straining food out of
the ocean.

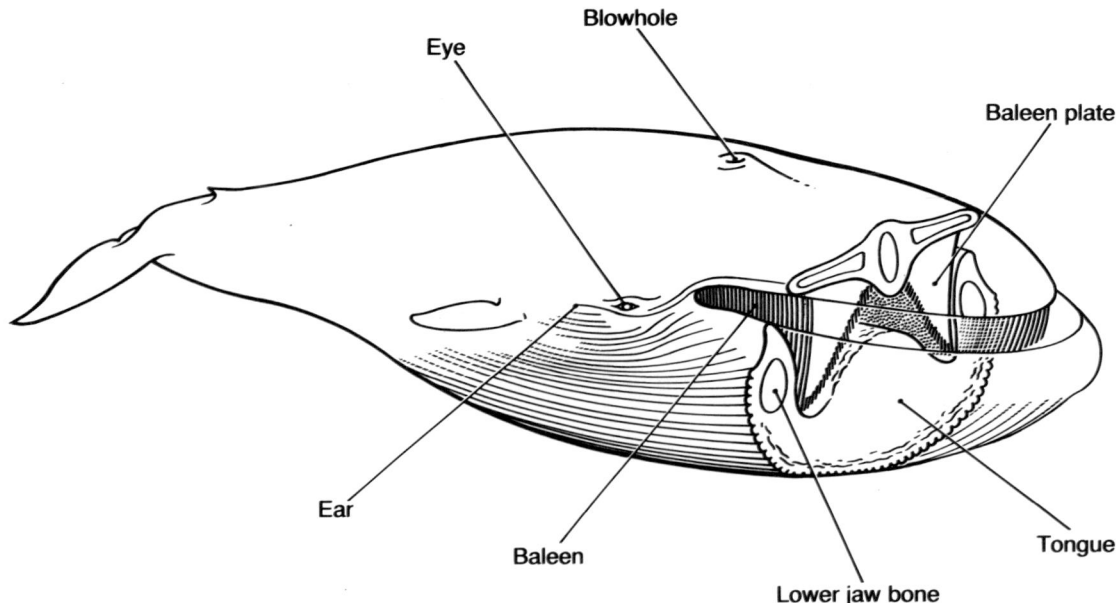

Eye

Blowhole

Baleen plate

Ear

Baleen

Lower jaw bone

Tongue

in krill or other suitable food they open their mouths and appear to take bites. The mixture of water and food is then squeezed as the throat grooves tighten up and the tongue is raised to reduce the size of the mouth cavity. The water escapes through the 2–3cm (1in) gaps between the baleen plates, but the food is caught on the interlocking fibres lining the mouth. The food can then be swallowed with rather little water remaining.

Fin Whales are known to roll onto their right sides as they approach a swarm of krill or school of fish. With open mouth and bulging throat the whale turns on the right flipper, scooping up the food. The lop-sided colouring on the head, with more white on the right, probably acts as camouflage in this movement, as the fin whale is white underneath to make it less easy to see from below.

The Right and Bowhead Whales feed by skimming off the food organisms from the water. They swim along with the mouth open wide, so that the water is filtered continuously until enough food has been collected and can be swallowed. Sei Whales feed at different times both by gulping and skimming. The Right and Bowhead Whales do not have throat grooves, but they have enlarged the size of their mouths by a great development of the head and jaws which arch to contain baleen plates up to 2m (6½ft) in length. The baleen is fine, and the main food is small plankton.

The baleen fringes of Blue Whales on the other hand are fairly coarse, so they rely almost completely on the larger animals for their food. They take little but krill in the Antarctic, and similar food in the North Atlantic and North Pacific. Fin Whales have a slightly finer baleen filter, and so can trap rather small species, as well as krill in the Antarctic. In the Northern Hemisphere they also eat fish such as herring, cod, mackerel and capelin. Sei Whales have a similar diet, although with an even finer baleen sieve they can capture smaller

The inner surface of the baleen plates of the Sei Whale shows the mat forming the sieve of fine hair-like fringes.

Opposite: Water streams from either side of the mouth of a Humpback Whale as it lunges to feed in Glacier Bay, Alaska.

animals as well. Minke Whales live mainly on fish, especially in the Northern Hemisphere, and eat squid and krill in the Southern Hemisphere. Bryde's Whales are also predominantly fish eaters, and have coarse baleen well suited to a diet of larger organisms such as sardines, mullet and anchovy.

The Humpback Whale has baleen which is coarse and stiff, best suited for gulping larger shrimps and fish. Off Alaska they have developed a special technique to concentrate the fish schools. The whale dives about 15m (50ft) below the surface and swims in a circle. As it does so, it releases a stream of air through the blowholes, which spirals upwards like a net of bubbles to herd the fish together. The whale then lunges upwards open-mouthed through this mass of food.

The Gray Whale is unique among the baleen whales because it feeds on the bottom of the shallow coastal seas it frequents. The diet consists mainly of small crustaceans which it stirs up from the mud with its snout, and then strains out through the baleen. As a result the food swallowed is mixed with quantities of sand, mud, pebbles and other organisms. This habit of grubbing on the bottom for food has also given rise to the slightly inaccurate alternative name of "mussel digger".

The chief food of Sperm Whales is squid, although fish make up a major part of the diet in some areas such as Iceland, New Zealand and in the North Pacific. The squid eaten are usually about 1m (3ft) long, although giant squid up to 10.5m (34ft) have been swallowed. The food is usually taken close to the ocean floor or in mid-water, but not at the surface, and swallowed whole. How the Sperm Whale finds its prey in the blackness of the ocean depths is not certain, but it probably relies on echolocation to detect and identify the food. It may also stun the squid or fish by a powerful blast of sound generated in the large head and focussed through the oil-filled spermaceti organ. The food can then be seized in the jaws, where the large teeth prevent its escape before it is passed down the throat.

A curious substance found in the Sperm Whale intestine is *ambergris*. It is dark and waxy-looking when fresh, but lighter in colour as it dries and has a rather musky smell. It has been known and used since ancient times as a medicine and until recently it was in great demand as a fixative in expensive perfumes, helping to bind the scent in the liquid. Ambergris from the Sperm Whale often has the beaks of squid and other hard parts of food embedded in it, showing its origin. Small pieces of ambergris weighing up to 10kg (22lb) are found floating in the sea or washed ashore after they have passed through a whale. More spectacularly, a lump weighing 455kg (1,003lb) was found in a Sperm Whale caught off Tasmania in 1912. Another weighing 420kg (926lb) was found in a Sperm Whale in the Antarctic in 1953.

A Southern Right Whale lifts its tail flukes off South Georgia in the sub-Antarctic.

Living in the Ocean

Swimming

The whale beats its large tail flukes up and down rather slowly. This displaces a large volume of water at a comparatively slow speed, leading to highly efficient swimming. The flattened tail flukes provide the main forward movement during their up-thrust, with the down-stroke as a more relaxed, recovery stroke. The largest muscles in the body are those running down the back of the whale, so that when these contract they draw the tail up strongly and the animal is pushed forward as water is drawn over the head and chest. In the downward recovery movement the tips of the flukes curl upwards and spill the water sideways. The whale glides forward between the up and down movements of the tail. If the animal is swimming fairly close to the surface, the tail movements produce a characteristic "slick" of oily-smooth water from the force of the upstroke.

Whales have lost the coat of hair which covered their land-living ancestors, leaving smooth bare skin which helps to reduce friction as the body moves through the water. The skin of a whale is quite flexibly attached to the body. The flow of water over the body follows a special pattern as the whale moves forward. The skin responds to this flow by flexing and moving in a way which reduces the drag and friction which would occur over a more rigid shape. This combination of flow and body form results in a very efficient swimming movement, and allows the whale to travel at speed with the minimum of effort.

Blue Whales commonly swim at 8–10 knots, ($14\frac{1}{2}$ – $18\frac{1}{2}$km/h:9 – $11\frac{1}{2}$mph) but they can spurt to twice this speed for up to 10 minutes if frightened or otherwise stimulated. Fin Whales are one of the fastest of the great whales, and up to 20 knots (37km/h:27mph) can be achieved in short bursts. On the spring migration, Fin Whales cover some 3,850km (2,400 miles) in a month from the breeding grounds to the Antarctic, or about 145km (90 miles) a day. A Fin Whale tagged with a radio transmitter was followed at an average speed of 9km/h ($5\frac{1}{2}$mph). A radio-tagged whale travelled 2,100km (1,300 miles) in 10 days between Iceland and Greenland, covering 292km (182 miles) in one day. The Humpback Whale is slow compared with the other roquals. It generally cruises at about 4 knots (7.5km/h – $4\frac{1}{2}$mph), although it can reach speeds up to 13 knots (24km/h – 15mph).

Diving

Although they are air-breathing animals, and must come to the surface to take in fresh air, whales do spend a lot of their time below the sea surface. Most of the baleen whales

A "slick" of smooth water marks the beat of the tail of a Humpback Whale just below the surface.

Above: A Fin Whale surfaces in the Denmark Strait between Greenland and Iceland.

Right: This photograph of a Sperm Whale underwater captures the movements of the tail and body as it swims.

Opposite: The forelimbs of the Gray Whale help to steer and control the body as it swims through the sea lower side up.

probably do not dive very deeply, or stay below the surface for very long. Since most of their food is found in the upper layers of the sea there is little need for them to do otherwise. Blue Whales do not usually dive more than 100m (325ft) deep, but it is believed that they can go down to 500m (1,625ft).

The Sperm Whale, however, feeds on animals found in the depths. Sperm Whales have been found entangled in telegraph cables on the sea floor at depths of 1,000m (3,250ft) or more. It seems almost incredible that an animal can withstand the pressure which presses on its body at such depths. For every 10m (32ft) the whale dives below the surface the water pressure increases by

one atmosphere, so the whales caught in the submarine cables were under some 100 atmospheres pressure.

Sperm Whales when they are feeding usually stay below the surface for up to one hour. Modern whaling vessels are fitted with underwater sound scanning equipment for echolocation, and with this apparatus it is not unusual to find Sperm Whales descending to depths of more than 1,000m (3,250ft) on such long dives. Even newborn whales have been tracked down to 650m (2,000ft) in dives lasting 17 minutes.

The greatest depth reported for a Sperm Whale dive comes from two animals which submerged for 1 hour 52 minutes and 53 minutes respectively, caught together in the Indian Ocean off Durban in August 1969. One of these whales was found to have swallowed two small bottom-living sharks. The depth of the sea floor in that area is over 3,000m (10,000ft).

How does a whale manage to survive at such depths? When a human diver descends below the surface he continues to breathe, and at depth the increased pressure results in large amounts of nitrogen from the air in the lungs becoming dissolved in the blood and tissues. When the diver returns to the surface he must do so slowly to prevent the nitrogen forming bubbles of gas as the pressure lessens. If this does happen it causes the painful and dangerous condition known as the "bends" when the bubbles are trapped and expand in the joints.

When a whale dives, it does not continue to breathe, and in addition the lungs are relatively small compared with the size of the body. The animal is able to cope with this amount of air quite easily, particularly since the chest and lungs are designed to collapse under pressure. This forces the air into the rigid windpipe, which helps to reduce the absorption of gases into the blood.

The tissues in the whale's body are also especially developed to take up oxygen. The muscles contain large amounts of myo-

The twin blow holes on the top of the head of the Gray Whale are closed just before it dives.

globin, a protein which can combine with oxygen and store it ready to be burned up as energy is required. In Sperm Whales this gives the meat a very dark, almost black appearance. Other whales which do not dive for so long or so deeply have a paler coloured meat. Whales are also able to withstand the build-up of carbon dioxide and other waste products such as lactic acid which are formed when energy is used. In addition, the animal can build up a considerable oxygen debt while continuing respiration in the absence of oxygen (*anaerobic respiration*). The blood supply continues to the brain and heart, but is reduced to other parts of the body, and the heartbeat slows during a dive. The blood system contains a number of intricate networks of vessels embedded in the fat. These are thought to act as blood reservoirs for use during the pressure changes which

accompany diving. In these various ways the whale is well adapted for remaining submerged for long periods and tolerating the stresses placed on the body at depth.

Breathing

The blowhole, or nostril, of all whales has moved from the normal position at the front of the head in a land mammal to the top of the head. This is an especially important adaptation for an air-breathing animal living in the sea. The whale can get rid of the stale air in its lungs and replace it with fresh as soon as the top of the head breaks the sea surface. The jet of pent-up breath contains a little of the oil film lubricating the membranes of the nasal passages and also water droplets carried up by the air rushing out as the whale surfaces. This mixture of air and liquid forms the characteristic *blow* or *spout* of the whale and hangs in the air for several seconds as the warm breath condenses, even in tropical seas.

The size and appearance of the blow, which varies from species to species, can help to distinguish the different kinds of whales. All the baleen whales have a double opening to the blowhole, representing the twin nostrils found in most mammals. Their spout is a vertical jet of variable height and bushiness depending on the kind of whale concerned.

The blow of a Blue Whale can be as much as 9m (30ft) high, slender and vertical. The Fin Whale's blow is more bushy, 4–6m (13–20ft) high and shaped like an inverted

The strong blast of stale air from the Sei Whale's lungs makes a distinctive bushy blow.

29

Early whaling in the Arctic was carried out by hand harpoon from open boats to extract the oil from the blubber, as well as to collect the long baleen plates of the Right Whales.

cone, and the other rorquals are similar but smaller. Right whales are clearly identified by having a V-shaped spout up to 5m (16ft) high.

The breathing pattern is rather more regular in the Sei Whale than in some other rorquals. Blows occur at 20 to 30 second intervals followed by a dive for up to 15 minutes or longer.

The Sperm Whale is like the other toothed whales in having only a single blowhole. But this is set well over to the left and towards the front of the head, so that the blow is directed forward at an angle as the whale surfaces. The generally bushy spout is usually less than 2.4m (8ft) high.

Blubber

The skin of a whale is actually very thin, only a few layers of cells thick, but underneath is a very much thicker layer of blubber. Blubber is made up of tough and fibrous tissue and much fatty material which acts as an important store of food. The baleen whales on the polar feeding grounds build up a thick layer of blubber during the summer months. This becomes noticeably thinner after the whales migrate to the breeding areas in the warmer tropical seas, where they eat rather little and use up some of their stored food reserves. A female whale which is feeding her calf with milk

draws on the food store in the blubber and it is relatively lean compared to a pregnant animal which builds up the fat reserves ready for birth.

Another function of the blubber is to act as an insulating blanket, and prevent too much body heat from being lost into the surrounding sea. Body temperature is regulated in part through a network of blood vessels which pass through the blubber to the skin. If surplus heat has to be lost, when increased activity by the whale has warmed the body too much, these blood vessels enlarge. They are especially abundant in the tail flukes, the flippers and fin, where the blubber is thinnest and most heat can be carried from the body by way of the blood to the sea. At other times heat may

need to be retained in the body. Then the surface blood vessels close and heat is transferred between the arteries near the surface and the veins which surround them, so that the heat is returned to the centre of the body without too much loss.

Sounds

Whales live in a world of sound. They can see both above water and below the surface, but sight is not so important a sense to them as it is to many terrestrial mammals because light does not penetrate very far into the ocean. In addition, the position of the eyes on the sides of the head of the great whales limits the field of vision which they can scan with both eyes together. Water, though, is a

The blubber is a valued product of the Bowhead Whale taken by modern Eskimos in Alaska, a delicacy known as "muktuk".

31

The ear of the Fin Whale appears as a small indentation on the surface of the head behind the eye (at the end of the light streak on the left).

very good conductor of sound, and the whale is able to hear a very wide range of sounds which penetrate directly from the water into the head. There is no need for whales to have external ear flaps such as a land animal requires to concentrate the sounds travelling in air.

Most species of whale create sounds for a variety of purposes. Large baleen whales such as the Blue Whale produce mainly the lower frequencies, which are deep notes capable of travelling great distances across the oceans. Such deep sounds are just within the human range of hearing. Most are made in association with some kind of social activity between the whales. Solitary whales are usually silent. The length of the sound varies from a half-second call in Minke Whales to more than 20 seconds in the Blue Whale.

Fin Whales can also emit sounds over a wider frequency as well as the typical low notes. The higher frequency sounds appear to be used for communication between nearby Fin Whales, and lower sounds for both local and longer distance communications. Some of these lower sounds are produced in patterns during courtship displays, at least in the western North Atlantic.

Probably the best known sound produced by a whale is the song of the Humpback, which has appeared on records and in films. It makes a wide variety of noises which range from low "snores" to high "chirps". Single units of sound are combined into sequences or phrases which in turn are combined into longer themes. It seems that only the male Humpbacks produce these songs, when they are near the winter

Humpback Whales swimming together can communicate by sounds in order to pass on information and keep in touch.

breeding grounds. All the Humpback Whales in the same area produce the same song and repeat it over and over again. The sequences may extend from 5 to 30 minutes and the Humpback can continue to sing for many hours on end. One animal has been recorded singing continuously for 22 hours. The song changes slowly during the breeding season, and also from one year to the next, but it still contains some recognizable elements over long periods of time. Some whales can be identified by their song.

Such complicated sounds are clearly used for communication between individual animals. In the case of the Humpbacks, the song advertises the presence of the males on

the breeding grounds to the females, and perhaps deters other males from approaching too closely.

The sounds may also help the whale to find its way about in relation to the sea bed and surface, although echolocation is usually best achieved through high energy clicks. The Sperm Whale makes a lot of these sounds, and it is likely that it can pinpoint objects around it with great accuracy from the returning echoes of these clicks. This is especially important when hunting prey such as squid which have a very fast escape reaction, or fish, in the inky blackness of the depths where the Sperm Whale feeds.

33

The Fin Whale calf
grows to about half
the length of its
mother by the time it
is weaned at the age of
six months.

The Life History of Whales

The whole life cycle of the rorquals is geared to the regular seasonal migrations. The whales mate in the warm temperate waters of both Northern and Southern Hemispheres in the winter months. The female generally carries a single foetus for a year or a little less, depending on the species. This means that while the baby whale is growing inside its mother, she has migrated to the colder polar waters and built up a good food store in her blubber and body. The mother then returns to the breeding grounds once more to give birth nearly a year later.

Although breeding and giving birth can occur at almost any time of the year in rorquals, it is largely confined to a relatively short peak period. Most Fin and Sei Whales in the Southern Hemisphere become pregnant between April and August, and most Blue Whales there are born in May and June.

Breeding behaviour in the large whales has not been seen very often except in species such as the Humpback Whale which tend to come close to the coast at this time. Humpback Whales mating can be an impressive sight. The male and female dive and swim towards each other at speed. Just before they meet they turn upwards and leap above the surface of the sea with their

A whale which has escaped an attack is often marked by the teeth of Killer Whales, as the tail of this Humpback shows.

The Sperm Whale calf is very soon able to swim and dive after it is born, as this 4m (13ft) new-born baby shows in the Indian Ocean.

undersides pressed together. The splash as they fall back into the water can be heard miles away. Most whales, though, mate rather less vigorously, lying together at the surface, stroking one another with their flippers and rubbing against each other before they couple.

Unlike mammals that live on land, the whale gives birth to its baby tail first. This allows the whole of the body to be free from the mother before the head emerges and the calf has to take its first breath of air. The newborn baby is often pushed to the surface by its mother, or another whale which may be standing by to assist at this time.

Because of their size, the great whales do not seem to have many natural enemies. A healthy adult whale is probably protected by its size, and smaller whales in groups should not be liable to attack. However, Killer Whales and sharks may be a danger to female whales when they are giving birth. The very young newborn animals are also especially at risk. Killer Whales and sharks have been seen around a group of Sperm Whales when one of them was giving birth. On three occasions when Sperm Whales have been observed giving birth in the open ocean, the mother has been in the centre of a circle of other whales. The other Sperm Whales were thrashing their tails and moving around the mother and her calf when it emerged at the surface and appeared to act as a defence at this time. Injured or sick animals are also at risk from these predators, since they are not so well able to defend themselves by a blow from the tail or a snap of the jaws. It is not unusual to find a few large whales with teeth marks or small pieces of the flippers or flukes missing where they have escaped from an attack.

The protective behaviour shown by a female towards her calf may turn into aggression towards any boat or other threatening object which approaches too closely. In the case of the Gray Whales in the breeding lagoons of Baja California this earned them the name of "devil fish" from the old whalers and a reputation for ferocity.

At birth the Blue Whale calf is 7m (23ft) long and weighs $2\frac{1}{2}$ tons. It feeds on its mother's milk for about 6 months, and grows very quickly during this time while the whales are starting on their spring migration to the polar feeding grounds. The milk from a female whale is very rich, and is pumped by muscles along the mother's belly out of the two mammary glands into the mouth of the calf as both whales swim together at the surface. By the time the whales have reached their summer grounds and the calf is ready to start eating krill on its own, the baby Blue Whale has grown to a length of 16m (52ft) and a weight of 23 tons.

The young whale continues to grow rapidly for the next few years, gradually becoming independent of its mother. It is characteristic of the rorquals that they start to breed when they have reached a certain body size, which is most conveniently measured in terms of length. For example, female Blue Whales in the Southern Hemisphere can start to reproduce when

A Gray Whale mother is very protective towards her young calf, and keeps it close beside her during its early life.

A young Blue Whale calf jumps playfully beside its mother.

they are about 23.5m (77ft) long, and female Fin Whales when they are 19.8m (65ft) in length.

The numbers of all these whales have been reduced in the past by hunting. Before this happened, about 50 years ago, the Fin Whales reached the critical size for breeding when they were around 10 years old. Now, however, because the smaller number of whales remaining have relatively more food each to eat, they grow more quickly and reach this size after only 6 years.

Once they have become sexually mature, the whales follow the regular cycle of mating and calving so that they can produce a calf every two years.

There are records of more than one foetus being found in a whale, and twins occur about as frequently as in humans, that is seven or eight in every thousand pregnancies. It seems unlikely that a whale mother could safely deliver more than one baby of such a size, and would find it even more difficult to feed them both during the period of very rapid early growth.

The baleen whales tend to form rather loosely associated groups which become more firmly structured during the breeding season. At this time particularly there is often an outburst of intense social activity.

Blue Whales are usually solitary or occur in pairs, although small groups and even

Humpback Whales are very acrobatic, and despite their bulk they can leap clear of the water in a formidable show of power.

The leap ends in a resounding splash of spray and foam as the Humpback Whale crashes back into the sea.

The long fore flipper of the Humpback Whale is often raised above the surface of the sea, where it may be gently waved or slapped down on the surface.

three are usually a mother and calf with an escort whale. Humpback Whales in particular are well known for their very spectacular and acrobatic displays. Despite their apparently rather solid and robust shape, they are quite agile and can thrust parts or all of the body above the sea surface. The most exciting of these movements is known as "breaching". The whale jumps almost completely out of the water and may twist in the air to drop back on its side or back. Such behaviour is also seen quite often in Minke Whales, which can leap and arch over so that they re-enter the water head first.

Humpback Whales quite often slap the surface of the sea with their long flippers. The sound produced can be heard over long distances and may be a form of communication between neighbouring animals. Slaps are also made with the tail flukes by a number of species. This is called "lobtailing", and most baleen whales do it at one time or another. The whale appears to stand on its head to carry out this manoeuvre. It swishes the tail above the surface of the sea and then splashes the wide flukes down with a loud report.

Gray Whales in particular can stand with their head lifted clear of the water in a position called "spy hopping". Rapid beats of the tail bring the eyes above the sea surface and the whale appears to survey its surroundings, often turning to scan the area around it for up to 30 seconds. It may behave in this way both in the breeding lagoons at the southern end of its migration path and in the ice floes of the northern feeding grounds.

Sperm Whales have a four- or five-year interval between each birth. The whales mate in spring, when the solitary big males join the mixed schools of adult females, some already with their calves, and juvenile whales of both sexes. The calves are born after a pregnancy lasting 15–16 months, when they are 4m (13ft) long and weigh about 1 ton. The Sperm Whale calf feeds on her mother's milk for at least two years.

aggregations of forty to fifty have been seen together. Similarly, although Fin Whales are sometimes found singly or in pairs, they commonly form groupings from three to twenty which may in turn join up into a broadly spread concentration of a hundred or more individuals, especially on the feeding grounds. Sei Whales are usually found in groups of up to half a dozen individuals, although on the feeding grounds there may be larger numbers associated together.

Humpback Whales are seen in ones, twos or threes, or in groups of up to twelve. The pairs of animals are either a mother and her calf or a male and a female. The groups of

A Gray Whale looks around the breeding lagoon off the coast of Mexico – a behaviour that is known as "spy hopping".

There is then a very extended weaning period as the calf takes both solid food and milk. The females and juvenile whales stay in the temperate waters all year round. As food is present all the time there is not the same cycle of migration and feeding in sperm whales which is a feature of the rorquals.

The female Sperm Whales can start to breed when they are 9 years old and 9m (30ft) long. Females tend to stay together for a number of years, but the males start to segregate themselves shortly after weaning and form their own groups. These bachelor groups then break up as the animals begin to mature. This process happens slowly in the males, and is not complete until they are 20 years old. The males are then 12m (39ft) in length, but they continue to grow slowly for another 10 years before they are big enough at 13m (43ft) and sufficiently socially mature to mix and mate with the females.

The total life span of whales is generally similar to that of people. Measured by the number of growth layers in a horny plug which forms part of the internal structure of the ear, Fin Whales can reach a maximum age of 90 years or a little more. The age of Sperm Whales can be judged from the growth layers in the dentine of the teeth. The maximum age reached in this species is around 60 years or a little more.

41

The Conservation of Whales

In the relationship between whales and humans the whales have generally suffered very badly. They have been seen as a source of food and other products for many centuries and hunting has spread from the coasts out across the open oceans. As a result nearly all the species of large whales have been much reduced in numbers. Fortunately, the most depleted populations are now given protection through international agreements from further commercial hunting, so that they have a chance to rebuild their numbers.

Whale products have formed the basis of subsistence for some native peoples and they are still permitted to catch a certain number, even though some of the whale populations concerned are depleted by earlier commercial catching.

The Eskimo communities in half a dozen villages around the north and west coasts of Alaska have a centuries-old tradition of hunting Bowheads. They still use sealskin boats launched from the ice-edge to pursue the Bowheads as they migrate along the leads in the sea ice in the spring, or migrate back again in the autumn. The weapons used to kill the whales are basically 19th century hand harpoons and shoulder guns, with some more modern refinements to improve efficiency. Once the whales have been killed they are hauled up onto the ice by the whole community. The cutting up and distribution of the meat and other parts of the animal are still organized and controlled in time-honoured fashion, with considerable ceremonial and cultural elements attached to the process.

Eskimo communities in Alaska catch Bowhead Whales for subsistence purposes. The whale is generally hauled on to the ice to be cut up in traditional fashion.

The native Aleut peoples of Siberia catch Gray Whales, but the Soviet authorities have provided a modern whale catcher for this purpose with normal commercial-style harpooning equipment. This allows a more efficient catch rate to be achieved than was possible with the traditional open boats and hand harpoons. The meat and products of the whales are eaten by the villagers and also used to feed the mink which they raise for fur.

Native Greenlanders also hunt whales from their dual purpose fishing and whaling boats armed with a small harpoon cannon on the bow. This kill is part of the whole subsistence hunt of these peoples, which includes fish, seals, birds and whales. The Greenlanders would prefer to catch Humpback Whales, but because the populations closest to hand are depleted, they have been persuaded to transfer their efforts to Fin Whales and Minke Whales.

In the meantime much scientific research is being carried out to learn more about the lives of the whales.

An especially important kind of study is the identification of individual whales in a particular population. One example is the case of the Humpback Whale, where the colouring on the underside of the tail flukes differs in pattern in each whale. Scientists now follow the Humpback Whales at sea and take photographs of the tails as they are turned up above the water just before a dive. Catalogues of photographs of recognizable individuals have been built up, and can be used to show that the Humpback Whales that spend the summer months off Greenland in the North Atlantic are the same animals that breed on the shallow banks off certain islands in the Caribbean during the winter. Similarly, whales photographed in summer off the coast of Alaska have been recognized around Hawaii or off the coast of Mexico in the North Pacific in the winter.

Right Whales too can be identified by the pattern of callosities on their heads. By recognizing the same animal over a number

The underside of a Humpback Whale tail has a unique colour pattern by which it may be distinguished.

of years it has been possible to find out such things as the interval between successive births. The growth of the mothers and of their calves can also be measured, as well as the relationships between the males as they come into the coastal breeding areas year after year.

Radio-tagging is another and more direct way of following the movements of a whale over the vast distances many of them cover in their annual migrations. Radio transmitters can be attached to the back of the whale, and these operate over considerable periods of time from their own batteries. The radio signal can be picked up from the shore if the whale keeps close enough, and Gray Whales have been followed in this way. Ships, aircraft or satellites can also be used to pick up signals from whales in the open ocean and so their movements are mon-

Whale watching has become an important industry, and here a boatload of tourists have a close view of a Humpback Whale in the Antarctic.

itored. The radio package attached to the whale is built in such a way that the signal identifying the animal is only transmitted when the aerial is above the surface of the sea. This conserves battery power, but means that the precise location of the whale is not known while it is submerged.

Research scientists are not the only ones interested in watching whales. In some parts of the world where whales come conveniently close to shore, there is an important tourist industry of whale watching. Small ships take passengers to areas where whales come regularly and so

Whales may be cast on the shore if they die at sea, as happened to this Minke Whale.

ordinary people can also enjoy all the varied behaviour of the whales.

Off the coast of California the migration of the Gray Whales to and from the breeding lagoons along the coast of Mexico is an exciting opportunity for whale watching from December to March each year. On the east coast of the U.S.A. whale-watching boats go out daily to see Right and Fin Whales in the area around Boston. Humpback Whales are readily seen by tourists from boats around the Hawaiian islands in winter as they congregate to mate and give birth.

Similar opportunities are available around Newfoundland, on the St. Lawrence River and Vancouver in Canada, in Japan and in Norway, and it is also possible to see whales from land where the animals come really close inshore. This occurs in Peninsula Valdes in Argentina where the Right Whales breed, as well as off the coast of South Africa.

Occasionally whales can be seen when they come ashore and strand. A whale may have died from accident or natural causes, and the carcase is washed up along with the other flotsam and jetsam of the ocean. In other cases the whale comes ashore alive. It has been suggested that live strandings occur when the animal enters shallow water and is deceived by confusing echolocation signals. Or it may be that the whale was so busy chasing fish or avoiding a predator that it did not take enough care about its own whereabouts. Stranded whales often contain many parasites in the brain and ear region, and it may be this infection that in some way caused the whale to strand. A further possibility is that the whale's navigation system, which seems to be sensitive to the Earth's magnetic field, has been confused by magnetic anomalies in the rocks in certain parts of the coast.

For whatever reason the animals come ashore, if they are found alive they must be kept wet while efforts are made to return them to the sea. Without the cooling effect of surrounding water the body temperature can rise dangerously high. In addition, the whale's skin is very sensitive to drying out and blisters easily in the sun, so it should be protected with damp cloths or wet sand. The blowhole should not be covered, though, for this would interfere with the breathing. It is often very difficult to return such stranded animals to the sea. The sheer physical difficulty of moving such a large body is a considerable problem. In the ocean the bulk of the whale is evenly supported by the surrounding water, but on land the skeleton is not designed to withstand the weight, and the internal organs and lungs are unnaturally compressed. Even when towed back to sea, some stranded animals refuse to swim to freedom, particularly if others of their group in a mass stranding are still ashore.

All in all, whales are fascinating creatures, beautifully adapted for their life in the sea. They can provide food and other products, but any hunting must be strictly limited to a level which the populations can sustain. Their behaviour and way of life is of great interest both to zoologists and to the general public, and they provide excitement and entertainment for all who can marvel at their size, grace, and beauty.

Above: A stranded Sperm Whale left in the shallows.

Left: Whale watching allows many people to experience the wonder of whales.

Index